Child Baker to Culinary Chef

Susan A. Tenteromano
and
Christopher E. Sanchez

Order this book online at www.trafford.com
or email orders@trafford.com

Most Trafford titles are also available at major online book retailers.

Printed in the United States of America.

ISBN: 978-1-4907-1921-4 (sc)
978-1-4907-1920-7 (e)

Library of Congress Control Number: 2013921464

Trafford rev. 03/13/2014

www.trafford.com

North America & international
toll-free: 1 888 232 4444 (USA & Canada)
fax: 812 355 4082

Christopher and Susan

of

Le Petit Bakery

Christopher and Susan hope their recipes and story of their baking will inspire the child and families as they bake together and find the joy of baking.

We share our recipes with you...
...We hope you will be inspired to perhaps go from childhood baker to culinary chef!

Contents

The book is crafted in the order of progression,
the stages of Christopher's growth of his baking skills.

Acknowledgment 4
Introduction 5
Safety in Cooking 6
Kitchen Hygiene 6
Tools 9

RECIPES

Sugar Cookie 11
Bishop Hats 13
Chocolate Almond Bark 14
Chocolate-Covered Pretzels 15
Walnut Tarts 17
Fingerprint Cookie 18
Swirl Cookie 21
French Almond Crescent Cookie 22
Italian Wedding Cookie 25
Raspberry Nut Bar 26
Lemon Squares 28
Sugar Twist Cookie 31

Shortbread-Shaped Cookies 32
Orange Citrus Cookie 34
Lemon Poppy Muffin 36
Coconut Macaroon 37
Chocolate Chunk 38
Linzer Tart Cookie 40
Madeline's for Madame 42
Nutter Butter 44
Oatmeal Cookies 46
Pizza Dough 47
Banana Bread/Muffin 49
Meringue Clouds 50

Resources and Helpful Hints 51
Measurement Conversion 52

Acknowledgment

When you are a young child you have your imagination open to so many possibilities. In all my years while growing up, various ideas for a career were thought of, such as an artist, an engineer, and as my grandmother had suggested a priest. Today, I am the chef and co-owner of Le Petit Bakery with my mom and we take great pleasure in writing this cookbook. I always imagined myself empowering a team of people, building something that people will appreciate knowing that it was accomplished with pride.

So here we are at Le Petit Bakery where families come together to enjoy our fresh pastries and breads, made from fresh wholesome ingredients. Susan and I want to thank our team at the bakery for their continued support as we grow and share our family's hospitality with a sense of welcoming into our home. We want to thank our sous chef Keelin Knapple; her dedication, professionalism, and continued support is inspiring and commendable. I want to acknowledge my sister Concetta who encouraged me to follow my childhood passion of baking by suggesting and locating a culinary school to attend. Today, Concetta continues to be supportive, giving of her time as well as offering her inspiring words "make it work"! A special appreciation to my wonderful wife Erika; she has supported me during the building of the bakery and continues to this day. Susan and I extend a special thank-you to Concetta Tenteromano, my grandma (Susan's mom) who made herself always available to help as we built our bakery and to this day in the kitchen.

Once again, we welcome you to enjoy our labor of love, our vision, our craft, and our recipes. We hope you enjoy the time baking as we have and hopefully you will continue for a long time.

Introduction

This book is a collaborative effort of Christopher and his mother, Susan. After years of working to perfect the family recipes, they have the desire to share those recipes with their friends, family, and newfound friends within the customers of Le Petit Bakery. Chef Christopher and his mom, owners of Le Petit Bakery, have been baking together since Christopher was two years old to the present day as Christopher is now the Pastry Chef of Le Petit Bakery. As the years went on, Christopher and his mom developed new recipes that are now a part of Le Petit Bakery. The love of baking grew from a childhood together time of "me and mom" to a tradition in baking together with family ever holiday. That enjoyment brings them to their present day business with the opening of Le Petit Bakery. The culmination of the following recipes will allow you to transcend into the creative mind of Christopher and Susan, as they take you through their experiences, pleasures and fun in discovering the joy of baking.

After years of developing the following recipes which were heavily guarded, Christopher and Susan will like to take you on their journey of baking. As you turn the pages through this book you will travel through time with Christopher as this book starts from his first desserts to present day new recipes of delight. They hope this book will offer you the insight to the love of baking and the enjoyment it brings to the table. Christopher and Susan experienced delight, fun, laughter, smiles, and joy of baking with family and friends, hoping you will do the same.

This book was published with a hope that families will develop the love of baking and be inspired to start a tradition in baking with family and friends.

They welcome you to discover the pleasure, the fun, the flavors and the delight in baking!

Safety in Cooking

Cooking is great fun and a time to create something that is totally yours to share with family and friends. Cooking involves multiple sharp tools and heat, so be careful and keep safety first. Think of your own safety and others around you by considering the following safety tips:

- Use gloves when handling hot items, such as trays and pots—everything out of the oven is *hot!*
- Do not put hot items on unprotected counter space. Use a heatproof mat, board, cooling tray, or a rack.
- When you are stirring food/liquids on the burner, grip the handle firmly to steady the pot.
- When cooking on a stove/burner (not stirring), turn the handle away from the heat and front to prevent accidents—less likely to knock into.
- Ask an adult for assistance when you are uncertain and need help. It's okay; we all need help!

Kitchen Hygiene

Safety and cleanliness go hand in hand; both are important in the kitchen. The following are a few ways to maintain a clean work area.

- Always, always wash your hands before starting to cook/bake, especially when handling raw meat/poultry products.
- Try to use colored cooking board designated for different type of food, such as green for vegetables, red for meat, yellow for poultry, blue for fish, and white for flour items.
- Wash all fruits and vegetables.
- Keep the cooking area clean and organized to avoid accidents and contamination.
- Always have clean clothes and paper towels handy to wipe spills.
- Check dates on all packaging—make sure they are not expired.

Tools

As you work through the kitchen and grow in this craft, you will need more and more baking/cooking tools. Listed below are some of the basic tools you will need to make the following recipes. Think of the basic tools around the kitchen you may possibly use.

- Cookie sheet
- Madeleine Pan
- Rubber spatula
- Ice Cream Scooper (small to medium)
- Whisk
- Electric mixer
- Measuring cup/measuring spoons
- Oven mitts/pot holder
- Rolling pin
- Clothes towel/paper towel
- Cutting boards
- Parchment paper
- Zester/grater
- Pastry brush
- Fine point paint brush

Invite a friend and have fun baking!

Start your own baking tradition!

Sugar Cookie

Ingredients

Flour – 2¼ cup
Sweet butter – 1 cup
Sugar – 1 cup
Egg – 1
Vanilla - 1 teaspoon
Salt – ½ teaspoon
Jelly/jam of your choice
Cookie cutter of your choice
Flour – small amount set aside for dipping the cookie cutter

Bake temperature: 325 degrees F
Bake time: 7–10 minutes
Yield: Varies on shape

Mixing instructions

- Cream together butter and sugar, then add egg, vanilla, and salt. Last, blend flour into a firm, soft dough.
- Roll out dough to approximately ¼-inch thick dough.
- Dip cookie cutter of your choice into a bowl of flour.
- Cut dough into your shape.
- Place on greased cookie sheet (can use parchment paper).
- Bake 7 to 10 minutes to a pale beige color.
- Cool and then decorate. Have fun!

Have a cookie-baking party. Invite a friend. Have fun!

Pick a shape and size

You are now royalty.

Bishop Hats

Ingredients

Cookie

Sweet butter – 3 sticks
Sugar – 1 cup
Flour – 4 cups
Eggs – 2 whole
Lemon – 2 teaspoons, finely shredded peel
Jelly/jam of your choice

Egg Wash - Used to seal edge of cookie.

Egg yolk – 1
Water – 1 tablespoon

Icing

Confection Sugar
Water or lemon flavor extract

Bake temperature: 325 degrees F
Bake time: 10 to12 minutes to pale beige
Yield: 35 round

Cookie Instructions

- Cream butter, sugar, and vanilla with mixer.
- Add flour slowly; use mixer partially.
- Add remaining flour and lemon peel.
- Knead together until smooth.
- Divide in half, wrap with plastic wrap. Chill for at least 1 hour.
- Roll dough into 1/8 inch thick.
- Cookie cutter – 3 inch rounds
- Dip cookie cutter into flour, then cut dough into 2-inch circles,
- Separate each circle; brush edge of circle with egg wash.
- Spoon jelly/jam in center of circle.
- Pinch the cookie, creating a three-side "bishop hat."
- Bake for 13 minutes at 325 degree F
- Cool, then drizzle with icing or melted dark chocolate

Chocolate Almond Bark

Ingredients

Chocolate melting chips – 16 oz
Whole almonds

Tools

Large pan
Silicone mat/parchment paper

Preparation Instructions

- Melt chocolate in double boiler pot (do not allow water to go into chocolate).
- Silicone mat on pan or parchment paper.
- Spread almonds evenly on the pan.
- Pour melted chocolate evenly over the almonds.
- Chill until firm.
- Break into desired sizes—varied sizes and shapes.

Enjoy the chocolate treat.
Simply delicious!

Chocolate-Covered Pretzels

Ingredients

Traditional pretzel – 2 bags (allowing for breakage)
Chocolate melting chips – 16 oz
(Milk chocolate, dark or white—your choice)
Sprinkles (optional)

Tools

Wax paper, flat tray (flat surface to hold pretzels)

Preparation Instruction

- Melt chocolate of your choice—use double boiler pot.
- Dip pretzel into chocolate.
- Lay each pretzel on wax paper.
- Sprinkles of your choice.
- Refrigerate until firm.

Be creative.
Make your own design.
Surprise a friend.

Walnut Tarts

Crust

Cream cheese – 6 ounces
Butter – 2 sticks
All-purpose flour – 2 cups

Bake temperature: Bake at 375 degree F for 10 minutes, then lower temperature to 325 degree F for an additional 10 minutes
Bake time: Total time 20 minutes

Yield: 35 round using a 3 inch cookie cutter
Pan: Mini cupcake pan

Mixing Instruction

- Cream butter and cream cheese to smooth; add flour to blend into smooth dough.
- Roll dough into 1/8 inch thick rounds to fit into each mini cupcake to form a mini crust for each tart. Use a 3 inch round cookie cutter.

Filling

Butter (soft) – 3 tablespoons
Brown sugar – 2¼ cups
Eggs – 3
Walnuts (chopped) – 2 cups

Mixing Instruction

- Cream brown sugar and butter until smooth and fluffy; add eggs one at a time then chopped walnuts, mix until completed blended
- Scoop a tablespoon amount into each mini crust.
- Bake at 375 degree F for 10 minutes, then lower temperature to 325 degree F for an additional 10 minutes.

Fingerprint Cookie

Ingredients

Sweet butter – 1½ cup
Brown sugar – ¾ cup
Vanilla – 1½ teaspoon
Egg yolk – 2 (Save the white for later.)
Flour – 3 cups
Choice of jelly/jam: strawberry, raspberry, apricot, etc.
Choice of nuts: walnuts, almonds, hazelnuts, etc.
White or Dark chocolate – optional (for drizzle on top of cookie)

Bake temperature: 325 degrees F
Bake time: 17 minutes
Yield: 30 cookies
(It should be light tan in color; check bottom for light brown.)

Mixing Instruction

- Cream butter and brown sugar, then add egg yolks, vanilla, and nuts.
- Flour—add one cup at a time until soft, creamy mixture is formed to hold a shape.
- Shape each cookie into a small round ball, approximately 1 inch round.
- Whip egg whites to a foamy consistency.
- Roll cookie into the egg white.
- Roll into finely chopped nuts of your choice.
- Place on a parchment paper lined pan; space an inch apart.
- Imprint the center to fill with jelly/jam of your choice.
- Bake, cool, drizzle chocolate (optional). Enjoy the eating!

Swirl Cookie

Ingredients

Eggs – 6
Sugar – 1 ¼ cups
Sweet butter – 2 sticks
Vanilla – 1 tablespoon
Baking powder – ½ cup
Orange – grate and squeeze 1
Lemon – grate and squeeze ½
Flour – 5 /2 cups

Bake temperature: 325 degrees F
Bake time: 12 minutes, should be pale in color, light tan on bottom.

Mixing Instructions

- Cream sugar and butter together, add eggs slowly then add all ingredients, except for flour.
- Add one (1) cup of flour at a time until mixed to a soft, sticky texture.
- Set aside in a bowl with a cloth cover for an hour to allow the dough to rise.

Shaping Instructions

- Roll a small amount into a piece ½ inch thick and 9 inch long piece for each cookie, and then swirl into a circular cookie starting from the center.
- Place each cookie on a cookie sheet lined with parchment paper.

Icing

- Confection Sugar – 1 cup
- Milk – enough to dissolve sugar for icing
- Optional – added flavor
- When cookies are cool, dip into icing, sprinkle with colored non-perils.

Great holiday cookie!
Enjoy the holiday with a great cookie!

French Almond Crescent Cookie

Ingredients

Sliced almonds - 1¾ cup
Sugar – ⅔ cup
Egg whites – 2, lightly beaten
Milk – 2 tablespoons
Flour – ¼ Cup – more as needed

Bake temperature: 375 degrees F
Bake time: 15 minutes
Yields: 15 to 18 cookies

Mixing Instruction

- Chop ¼ cup of almonds; set aside on flat plate.
- Finely grind 1½ cup of almonds.
- Stir sugar with ground almonds.
- Stir ⅔ of the egg whites and vanilla into sugar-almond mixture.
- Pour mixture onto floured board/counter. Kneed flour into mixture until the dough is workable to form a cookie shape.
- Flour hands to handle dough. Shape into approximately 1-inch ball. (dough will be soft)
- Shape each ball into a half-moon crescent shape.
- Brush with remaining egg whites; dip into chopped almonds.
- Arrange on parchment paper lined cookie sheet pan.
- Bake until light brown; brush with milk while warm.
- Place on cooling rack.
- Optional – dip one end of the cookie into melted chocolate

A cup of hot chocolate is awaiting you . . . enjoy!
Added chocolate to your to your hot chocolate!

Italian Wedding Cookie

Ingredients

Sweet butter - 2 sticks
Sugar - 6 tablespoons
Vanilla – ½ teaspoon
Walnuts – 1 cup
Salt – 1 pinch
Baking soda – 1 pinch
Flour - 2 cups

*Confection Sugar –Roll cooled cookie into the sugar.

Baking temperature: 325 degrees F
Bake time: 15 minutes, should be pale beige, bottom—light tan
Yield: 28 cookies (1 inch round)

Mixing Instruction

- Cream butter and sugar, then add chopped walnuts and remaining ingredients.
- Roll into small round balls (size optional).
- Bake on parchment paper lined pan
- When cookies are cool, roll into confection sugar

Not only for weddings so celebrate!

Raspberry Nut Bar

Ingredients

Sweet butter – 1 cup
Sugar – ⅔ cup
Eggs – 2
Hazelnuts – 1 cup
Flour – 4 cups
Egg wash – 1 egg beaten with water
Raspberry jelly/jam
Chocolate – 2 cups melted (Reserved for when the cookies are baked)

Bake temperature: 350 degrees F
Bake time: 10 to 12 minutes
Yield: varies with size

Raspberry Nut Bar

Mixing Instruction

- Cream butter and sugar, then add eggs.
- Add flour to blend together into soft dough.
- Divide into 2 parts. Wrap with plastic wrap. Refrigerate for at least 1 hour.
- Roll each part between wax paper into a rectangle, approximately 4 inches wide and approximately ¼ inch thick. Trim the sides to create rectangle shape dough.
- Brush ½ inch with egg wash along the wide side.
- Fold half of the egg washed side to seal together (egg wash allows the dough to be held together).
- Spread jelly/jam over the dough that is *not* folded.
- Sprinkle chopped hazelnuts over the jelly/jam.
- Bake – should be light tan.
- Cut the rectangle horizontally in half then vertically into 1-inch bar.
- Cool, dip the folded edge into melted chocolate.
- Dry on wax paper.

A rich tasting cookie, enjoy the flavors!

Lemon Squares

Ingredients

Crust

Sweet butter – 2 sticks
Flour – 2 cups
Confection Sugar – ½ cup

Filling

Eggs – 4
Sugar – 2 cups
Flour – 4 tablespoons
Lemon juice – 6 tablespoons
Pinch of salt - 1
Confection Sugar – sprinkle over top when finished baking

Directions for crust

Mix all ingredients, press onto a baking dish (9 x 13), bake for 15 minutes, remove from oven.

Bake temperature: 325 degrees F
Bake time: 20 to 25 minutes
Yield: varies with the size

Filling Instructions

- Beat eggs, then add one ingredient at a time (leave out the confection sugar); mix thoroughly, then pour onto baked crust.
- Cool; sprinkle confection sugar over top.
- Cut into squares.

Enjoy the sweet and sour taste!

Sugar Twist Cookie

Ingredients

Puff pastry - one box
Granulated sugar – enough for surface coverage of pastry

Tools

Rolling pin, wax paper

Bake time: 20 to 25 minutes
(should be light brown in color)
Bake Temperature: 375 degree F
Yield: 26 cookies

Assembly Instruction

- Cut a piece of wax paper to be larger than the size of the puff pastry.
- Sprinkle sugar on wax paper.
- Place one sheet of puff pastry onto the sugar and then place the second sheet of puff pastry onto the sugar (creating a sandwich).
- Cover with wax paper larger than puff pastry.
- With the rolling pin, roll over the two puff pastry pieces to flatten into one piece.
- Discard the wax paper.
- After rolling, cut 3/4 -inch strips of the puff pastry from the wide side
- Cut in half width wide
- Twist (one to three turns) creating a spiral
- Place on a parchment paper lined cookie sheet pan.
- Bake

Have fun baking. Enjoy!

Shortbread-Shaped Cookies

Ingredients

Butter – 2 sticks

Sugar – ½ cup

All-purpose flour – 3 cups

Bake temperature: 325 degrees F

Bake time: 10 to 15 minutes (depending on the size)

Check bottom—should be light beige.

Yield: varies with size and shape

Mixing Instruction

- Cream the butter and sugar.
- Add the flour to blend into a smooth dough
- Roll out between two pieces of parchment paper to approximately ¼ inch thick
- Cut out each piece with the cookie cutter f your choice

Shape into whatever you like.

Fly away with a butterfly, see the stars, or see the seashells.

Enjoy your designing, share your design, it is Art!

Orange Citrus Cookie

Ingredients

Eggs – 5
Orange juice – 1 cup, mix and set aside
Sweet butter – 2 sticks melted

mix and set

Flour - 6 cups
Baking powder – 4 teaspoons
Salt - 1 pinch
Sugar – 2 cups

Confection sugar – used for rolling cookie

Bake temperature: 375 degrees F
Bake time: 15 minutes, check color—should be pale beige

Mixing instruction

- Mix each section separately. (Do not add confection sugar to mixture.)
- Slowly mix the two parts together to blend completely.
- Use a small amount, shape into a ball approximately
- 1 ½ inch wide or smaller if you desire, the cookie rises
- Roll each cookie into a bowl of confection sugar.
- Place each cookie on parchment paper lined sheet pan
- Bake

Enjoy with tea or just by itself.
Mouthwatering!

Lemon Poppy Muffin

Ingredients

Butter – 2 sticks
Sugar – 3½ cups
Lemon zest – 2 lemons
Eggs – 2
Vanilla extract- ½ tablespoon
All-purpose flour – 4 cups
Baking powder – 1 teaspoon
Salt – 1 pinch
Baking soda – ¼ teaspoon
Poppy seeds – 4 tablespoons
Buttermilk – 3 cups

Glaze
Lemon Juice
Confection Sugar

Tools

Medium size scoop

Bake temperature: 325 degrees F
Bake time: 35 minutes, tops should be light brown

Mixing Instruction

- Cream butter, add sugar then lemon zest
- Slowly add eggs
- Add in dry ingredients, mix lightly
- Slowly add buttermilk
- Pour into regular-sized cupcake-lined cupcake pan.

Glazing Instruction

- Mix confection sugar and lemon juice to create glaze (should be clear thin texture)

Finishing the muffin

- After baked, cool, then brush with lemon glaze

Bake; enjoy the sweet lemony taste, warm or cold.

Coconut Macaroon

Ingredients

Coconut - unsweetened, shredded 10 ½ Cups
Sugar – 6 cups
Egg whites – 2¾ cups
Salt – 1 tablespoon
Dark Chocolate

Tools

Double boiler pot
1-inch deep cookie sheet

Bake temperature: 325 degrees
Bake time: 35 minutes
Yield: varies in size

Mixing Instruction

Takes 2 hours to cook to dry consistency,

- Mix sugar and egg whites over double boiler until the sugar is dissolved.
- Stir every 5 to 10 minutes until the mixture is dry, until the mixture sticks to the spatula and doesn't fall off
- Over low heat - Add coconut and salt.
- Mix well until all ingredients are blended.
- Pour onto parchment paper lined cookie sheet
- Bake
- Cool, cut into desired size and shape
- Melt chocolate over a double boiler
- Dip the ¼ side (corner) of the macaroon into the chocolate
- Place macaroon on parchment paper lined tray for drying.

Well, if you love almond joy, this is the cookie for you.
Now sit back and enjoy!

Chocolate Chunk

Ingredients

Butter – 2 sticks
Dark brown sugar – 1½ cup
Molasses – 2 tablespoons
Sugar – ¾ cup
Eggs - 2

Salt – ½ teaspoon
All-Purpose Flour – 2 ¾ cup
Baking soda – 1 teaspoon
61% chocolate - 1 cup, chopped
Chocolate chips – 1 cup

Bake temperature: 325 degrees F
Bake time: 16 to18 minutes

Mixing Instruction

- Cream the butter for 3 minutes.
- Add sugar to cream for another 3 minutes.
- Add eggs to cream mixture for 2 minutes.
- Add dry ingredients to cream mixture.
- Add chocolate to the mixture, combine all ingredients.
- Scope 1 inch cookies onto parchment paper lined pan
- Bake

Enjoy the Chocolaty Taste!

Linzer Tart Cookie

Ingredients

- Butter – 2 sticks
- Sugar – ¾ cup
- Vanilla extract – ¼ teaspoon
- Eggs - 1
- Almond flour – ¾ cup
- Hazelnut flour – 1 cup
- Cake flour – 2¾ cup
- Cinnamon – ⅛ teaspoon
- Baking powder – 2 teaspoons
- Orange zest – 1 orange

Filling

Raspberry preserves

Finishing touch

Confection sugar – dust on the top of the baked cookie

Bake temperature: 325 degree F
Bake time: 14 minutes for a 3 inch cookie cutter

Mixing Iznstruction

- Cream the butter for 3 minutes
- Add sugar and cream together.
- Slowly add the eggs and vanilla; blend well
- Add remaining ingredients; blend well.
- Shape into the size and shape of a sandwich cookie.
- This cookie is a two part cookie; the top cookie has a center cut out. With the cookie cutter of your choice, cut out a center whole of one of the two cookies (top cookie).
- Bake both parts of the cookie on a parchment paper lined pan.
- Cool cookies
- Spread a small amount of preserves on the bottom cookie (the one without the center whole), squish the top and bottom together.
- With a strainer, dust the cookies with confection sugar

This is not an Oreo, no separating the cookie!

Madeline's for Madame

Ingredients

Butter – 2 sticks
Dark brown sugar – 2 tablespoons
Honey – 2 tablespoons
Sugar – 1¼ cup
Eggs – 6

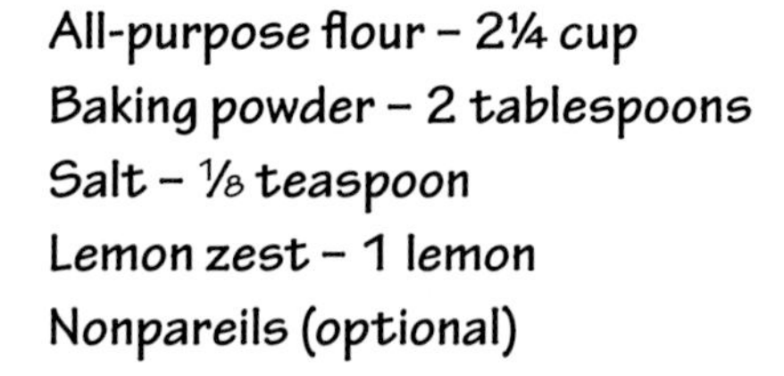

All-purpose flour – 2¼ cup
Baking powder – 2 tablespoons
Salt – ⅛ teaspoon
Lemon zest – 1 lemon
Nonpareils (optional)

Tools

A Madeline pan is needed for this recipe.

Bake temperature: 350 degrees F
Bake time: 10 minutes
Yield: 64 cookies

Mixing Instruction

- Melt butter and brown sugar and honey – set aside
- Mix sugar and eggs for 5 minutes
- Add dry ingredients to egg mixture to combine
- Stream in boiling butter mixture
- Set entire mixture aside to rest for two hours
- Pour mixture into Madeline pan.
- Place pans on a cookie sheet
- Bake
- Cool cookies, flip over, and enjoy!
- Optional – Sprinkle with Nonpareils on one side to create a seashell look

Nutter Butter

Ingredients

Butter – 2 sticks
Peanut butter – 1/2 cup
Sugar – ½ cup
Brown sugar – 1 cup
Vanilla extract – 1 tablespoon
Eggs - 1
Baking soda – 1 tablespoon
Baking powder – 1 teaspoon
All-purpose flour – 1½ cup
Oats – 1 cup
Peanuts, chopped – ¼ cup

Bake temperature: 325 degrees F
Bake time: 10–12 minutes
Yield; 22 sandwiches using a two inch cookie cutter

Cookie Mixing Instruction

- Cream the butter until it has the same consistency as creamy peanut butter.
- Add peanut butter. Mix well.
- Add sugars, cream thoroughly until all ingredients are blended (approximately 4 minutes).
- Add eggs and vanilla, slowly to incorporate completely.
- Add oats and mix for a minute, then the peanuts, until all is mixed.
- Mixture will be sticky.
- Roll out into ⅛ thickness; shape two per cookie.
- Place each cookie on a parchment paper lined baking sheet.
- Bake
- Cool prior to filling
- Cookie will be soft, set in refrigerator for firmness

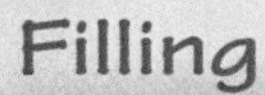

Filling

- Egg whites – 3 ounces
- Sugar – 8 ounces
- Sweet butter – 10 ounces
- Creamy peanut butter – 21 ounces

Filling Mixing Instruction

- Beat egg whites and sugar to fluffy peak
- Add soften butter, mix
- Add creamy peanut butter, blend well

Elephants love peanuts.
Make these cookies.
Go to the zoo.
Feed yourself and an elephant!

Oatmeal Cookies

Ingredients

- Butter – 2 sticks
- Brown sugar – 1 cup
- Sugar – ½ cup
- Eggs - 2
- Vanilla extract – 1 teaspoon
- All-purpose flour – 2 cups
- Baking soda – 1 tablespoon
- Ground cinnamon – 1 tablespoon
- Ground cloves – ½ teaspoon
- Salt – ½ teaspoon
- Oats – 2 cups
- Raisins – 1 cup

Bake temperature: 325 degrees F
Bake time: 15 minutes
Yield: 48 cookies using a 1 inch cookie cutter

Mixing Instruction

- Cream butter and sugar.
- Add eggs and vanilla.
- Add dry ingredients and raisins.
- Blend together and shape into your favorite shape of cookie!

Oatmeal is healthy for you;
these are yummy too!

Banana Bread/Muffin

Ingredients

Cake flour – 2 1/2 cups
Brown sugar – 1 ¼ cups
Baking powder – 1 teaspoon
Baking soda – 3/4 teaspoon
Salt – 1 teaspoon
Sour cream – 3 tablespoons
Eggs – 3
Vanilla extract – 1 tablespoon
Banana (mashed) – 1 ½ cups = approximately 4 bananas
Butter– 2 sticks

Bake temperature: 350 degrees F
Bake time: 35–45 minutes for a loaf pan

Mixing Instruction

- Cream butter and sugar
- Slowly add eggs
- Mix the flour, sugar, corn syrup, baking powder, baking soda, and salt.
- Add bananas, blend completely
- Mix well; add to greased pan or muffin pan with liners or loaf pans.
- Bake

Enjoy the Banana Taste...

...we prefer it warm!

Meringue Clouds

Ingredients

Egg whites – ½ cup
Sugar – 1 cup
Citrus zest (optional)
Nonpareils (optional)

Tool

Ice cream scoop or pastry bag with star tip

Mixing Instruction

- Heat sugar and egg white over a double boiler pot until dissolved
- Transfer sugars mixture to a mixing bowl (mixer) beat until the mixture forms a stiff peak
- Parchment paper lined tray, spray parchment with non-stick spray
- With a small ice cream scooper, scoop each cloud onto the sprayed parchment paper
- Allow to dry overnight in warm area or bake at 200 degree F for 40 minutes
- Optional—sprinkle nonpareils while wet.

The fluffy meringue allows you to imagine you are floating on a cloud make any shape, and decorate from the

Heart!

Resources and Helpful Hints

Places to purchase baking tools are as follows:

- www.bakedeco.com
- www.nycake.com
- www.williams-sonoma.com
- Ateco Products
- Amazon.com
- Sur La Table
- Your local bake ware store

Here are hints in baking:

- Read throughout the entire recipe.
- Set the work area with all the items you need—all the ingredients.
- Prepare the work space with clean towels, a pot holder, and trays.
- Preheat the oven.
- Use a timer.

Measurement Conversion

Cups	Fluid ounces	Tablespoons	Teaspoons	Milliliters
1 C	8 oz	16 tbsp	48 tsp	237 ml
3/4C	6 oz	12 tbsp	36 tsp	177 ml
2/3 C	5 oz	11 tbsp	32 tsp	158 ml
1/2 C	4 oz	8 tbsp	24 tsp	118 ml
1/3 C	3 oz	5 tbsp	16 tsp	79 ml
1/4 C	2 oz	4 tbsp	12 tsp	59 ml
1/8 C	1 oz	2 tbsp	6 tsp	30 ml
1/16 C	.5 oz	1 tbsp	3 tsp	15 ml

Printed in the United States
By Bookmasters